Sasha Pasha & Luna Moon
and some other little critters
Teamwork always wins
Copyright:
Gabriele K Soltau
Published July, 2018
All rights reserved.

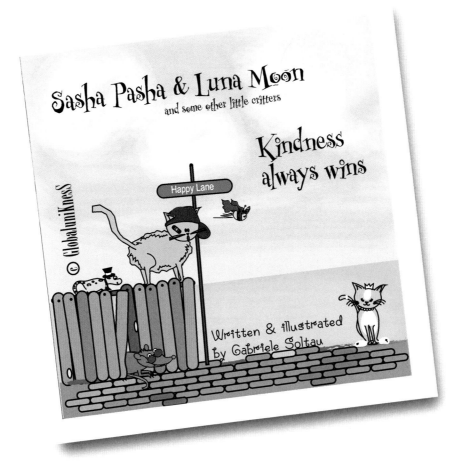

Also available: **Kindness Always Wins**
Volume 1 of this series, where some of the
adorable animal characters are introduced.

Sasha Pasha & Luna Moon

and some other little critters

Teamwork always wins

Dedicated to my great-nephew Robin Frederick

It was a sunny day in Love Town on Happy Lane as
Sassy, the squirrel was playing in the neighborhood.
The lady in the green dress was talking on her phone.
Because she was so distracted, she did not realize
that her car key slipped out of her purse.

Happy Lane

She kept chatting away and did not realize that she had lost her car key. Uh-oh...

Sassy, the squirrel was climbing the street sign pole
when she noticed a shiny object. It caught her attention.

Happy Lane

Sassy was fascinated with the shiny object
and picked it up.
Luckily Buzzy, the wonder-bee flew by and noticed
that Sassy had picked up the strange looking thing.

Sassy ran up her favorite tree with the shiny treasure.
She was going to hide it, so no one could take it from her.

Little did she know that birdie Robin was watching her.

In the meantime, as the sun was setting,
the lady in the green dress was
going to meet her friend for dinner.
That's when she noticed her car key was missing.
She was very worried and called her friend.

Buzzy overheard the conversation and was determined
to help. That's just what wonder-bees do.

Happy Lane

Her friend immediately came over and they both searched everywhere. They looked over the fence; they looked under the car. The key was nowhere to be found.

But Buzzy had a plan...

Happy Lane

Buzzy gathered her friends because she was aware that finding the shiny thing would require teamwork. Sasha, Luna, Leonard, and their new friend birdie Robin, were curious to hear what she had to say.
"Guys, we have to help the lady find the strange looking thing. I think she needs it for the big machine that she calls 'car'. And I think I know who took it!"

"And I think I know where she took it to", Robin chirped.

So everybody had ideas on how to recover
that weird looking thing that was needed
for the big machine called 'car'. Buzzy was afraid a fight
would break out. She knew teamwork was needed to get
the job done.

Page 9

"Stop it!" Buzzy got upset with them.
"Settle down! This is only going to work,
if we all work together as a team.
Let's meet tomorrow by the big tree!"

The next morning they
all gathered by the big tree.
Sassy was wondering
what in the world was going on.
She was ready to protect her
shiny treasure.

Sassy figured out they
had come to steal her treasure.
She threw a nut at them
and hit little Leonard in the
head. He fell over and his top-hat
toppled off.

Everybody was relieved that Leonard
was ok! So they met again to come up with a plan.
Buzzy had watched Sassy take the weird looking thing,
she was pretty sure it was somewhere by the tree.
And Robin was pretty sure it was inside the empty
nest way up in the tree.

The team was not going to give up.

The lady in the green dress and her friend were
both on the phone trying to figure out a way to
get another key.

They were utterly surprised when Sasha and Robin showed up. Their jaws dropped when the two told them that they were going to get that shiny, weird looking thing back to them.

So the plan was put in motion: Part 1 was for Robin to distract Sassy. He was going to show her a wonderful tree full of her favorite nuts.

It worked! He flew ahead of her to show her the way.

As soon as they were gone, part 2 of the plan was implemented: Sasha was going to climb up the tree, but little Luna was just a bit faster, so up the tree she went. Leonard was right behind her.

When Luna got close to the empty nest, she realized that she was too big to check out the inside. But Leonard was the perfect size!

Leonard easily fit into the opening. Everybody was eagerly waiting to see if the shiny object was indeed inside.

"Quickly! Drop it, Leonard!",
Luna shouted.

Suddenly - out of nowhere- Sassy showed up and ran up the tree. She almost caught the key, but birdie Robin

was quicker!

Sassy was a little upset:
"Hey you guys, can somebody
please explain to me what this
thing is? And why did you
take it from me?"

Buzzy said: "We don't really know
what it is, but the lady in the green
dress is desperately looking for it.
She needs it for the big red machine
that she calls 'car'." Sassy agreed to help.

So the whole group went to the lady's house and Sassy herself delivered the shiny object. The lady in the green dress and her friend were soooooo happy!

Now that the car key was finally found,
the lady and her friend took the whole gang for a ride.
It was her way of saying 'Thank you'.
Everybody had a great time.

WooHoo - Teamwork always wins!

Teamwork saved the day!

We all have different gifts and talents.
You may be really good with some things,
and your friend may be good with other things.
When we use our gifts and work together,
we can accomplish more than we would just by ourselves.

That's why Teamwork is so cool!

In our story, all the little animals worked together
and got the job done.

You have many gifts and talents. Use them to
help and bless others. No need to be jealous of anybody,
because you are uniquely wonderful.

The world needs you just as you are!

GlobaluniKnesS
© GKS 2018

Eternally Loved

66063525R00018